HART PICTURE ARCHIVES

American Designs

Under the General Editorship of
Harold H. Hart

Hart Publishing Company, Inc. • New York City

ISBN NO. 08055-0332-3
LIBRARY OF CONGRESS CATALOG CARD NO. 78-93871

MANUFACTURED IN THE UNITED STATES OF AMERICA

CONTENTS

HOW TO USE THIS BOOK

AMERICAN DESIGNS is a collection of over 400 pictures of many periods, culled from 24 known sources. These pictures have been subdivided into 11 categories.

All these pictures are in the public domain. They derive from magazines, books, and pictures copyrighted by Hart Publishing Company, now released to the public for general use.

So as not to clutter a caption, the source is given an abbreviated designation. Full publication data may be found in the *Sources* section, in which all sources are listed in alphabetical order, with the full title of the book or magazine, the publisher, and the date of publication. The *Sources* section commences on page 95.

A few of the pictures are halftones, and they are designated by a square symbol □ at the end of the caption. These pictures, too, are suitable for reproduction, but the user is alerted to rescreen such a picture or convert it into line. All other pictures can be reproduced directly in line.

Costa Rican Designs

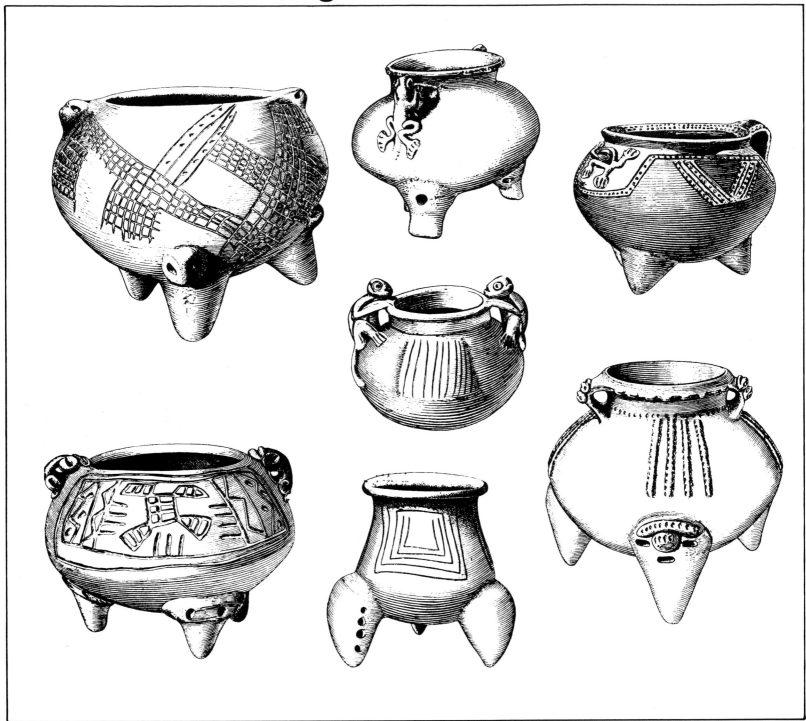

Coast Rican red ware. *Lothrop*

Whistle made from orange-brown ware, Costa Rica. *Lothrop*

Pottery rings from Costa Rica. *Lothrop*

Cylindrical stamp designs, Las Mercedes. *Lothrop*

Costa Rican chocolate ware. *Lothrop*

Costa Rican Designs continued

Pottery drum from the Nicoya peninsula. *Lothrop*

Costa Rican yellow-line ware, Las Mercedes. *Lothrop*

Three cylindrical stamps from the Nicoya peninsula. *Lothrop*

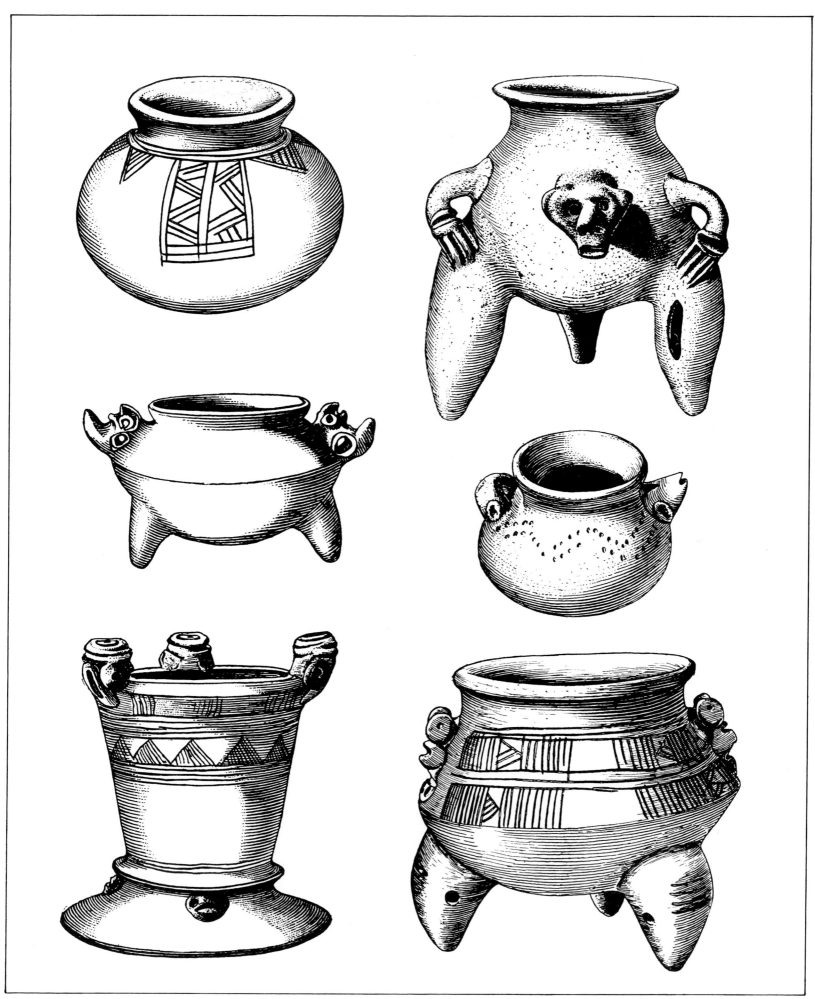

Costa Rican red ware. *Lothrop*

Early American Designs

Early 19th century quilt from Pennsylvania. *Source unknown*

19th century floral design. *Early American*

Early American Designs continued

Various embroidery motifs from an 18th century Massachusetts quilt. *Early American*

Various embroidery motifs from an 18th century Massachusetts quilt. *Early American*

Mexican Designs

Cylindrical stamp. *Design Motifs*

Earthen vessel from the Puebla state, Mexico. *Das Ornament Werk* □

Flat stamp from Azapotzalco. *Design Motifs*

Cylindrical stamp from Mexico City. *Design Motifs*

Variation on "blue worm" design. *Design Motifs*

"Covatl" or "serpent monster," Vera Cruz, Mexico. *Source unknown*

Aztec Design. *Source unknown*

Earthen vessel from Tlaxcala. *Das Ornament Werk* □

From a Mayan Manuscript.
Source unknown

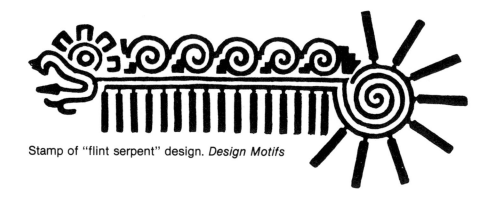

Stamp of "flint serpent" design. *Design Motifs*

Part of a mural painting from
Teotihuacan. *Das Ornament Werk* □

Mexican Designs continued

Aztec design. *Source unknown*

Vase from Vera Cruz, Mexico.
Das Ornament Werk □

Vase from Vera Cruz, Mexico.
Das Ornament Werk □

Facemask of serpentine from Guerrero,
Mexico. *Das Ornament Werk* □

Earthen vessel from the
Puebla state, highlands of Mexico.
Das Ornament Werk □

Earthen vessel. *Das Ornament Werk* □

Painting of parchment, Mixtec, Mexico. *Source unknown*

Mexican Designs continued

Mayan war-god. *Century*

Mexican earthen vessel. *Das Ornament Werk* □

Flat stamp from Mexico City. *Design Motifs*

Mayan vessel, Guatemala. *Das Ornament Werk* □

Floral design from Azcapotzalco. *Design Motifs*

Aztec design. *Source unknown*

Aztec design. *Source unknown*

Mayan rain-god. *Century*

Mexican Designs continued

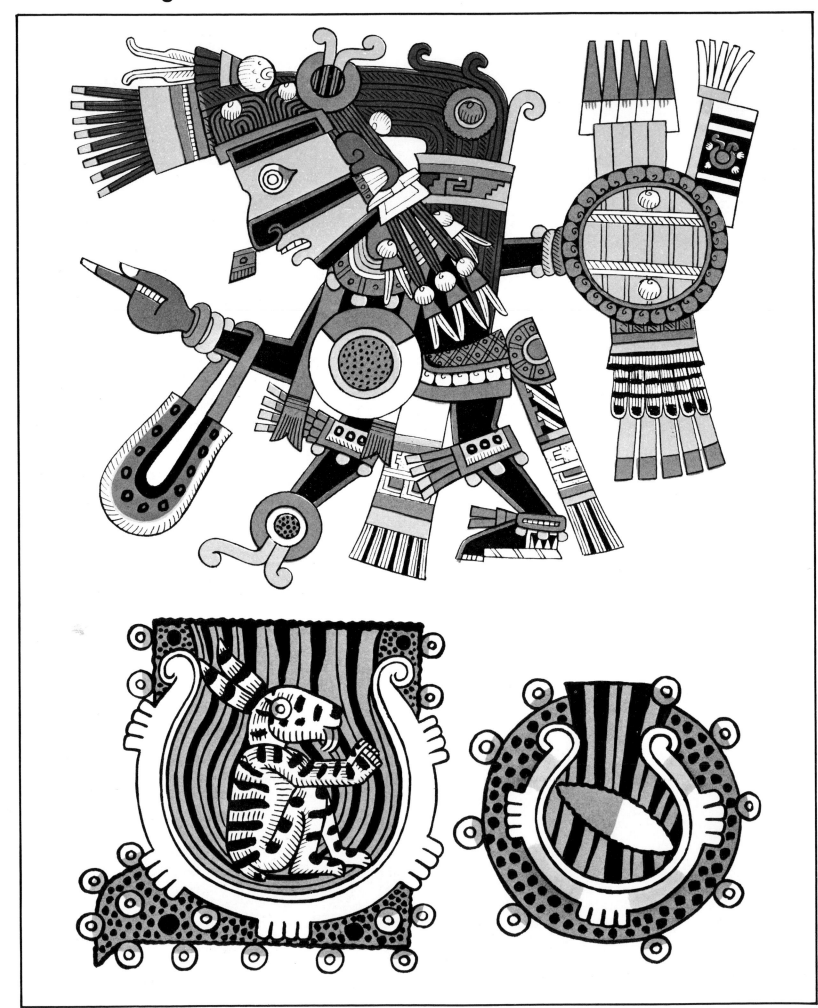

Tezcatlipoca *(top)* and two representations of the moon. *Source unknown* □

Mexican textile designs. *Encyclopédie* □

Modern Mexican tiles showing Aztec influence. *Source unknown*

Mexican Designs continued

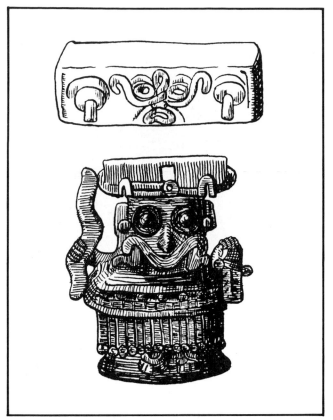

Mayan representations of *Tlalok* on pottery. *Origins*

Design showing dedication of the temple of *Huitzilipochtli*, the Aztec god of war. *Source unknown*

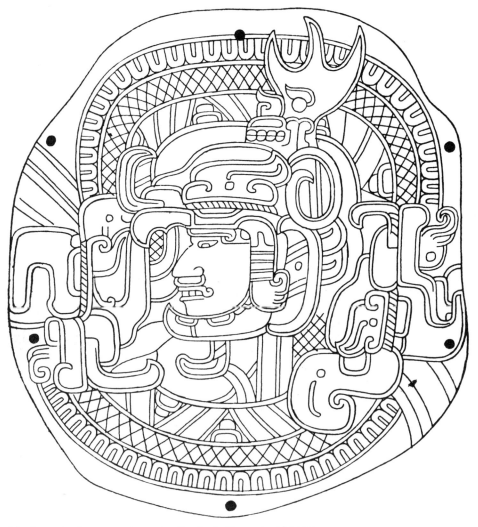

Mexican design carved on a turtle shell. *Source unknown*

Mayan vases found at Cuecuetenanco. *Incidents*

Figure of *Tlalok* on a piece of pottery from Quen Santo. *Origins*

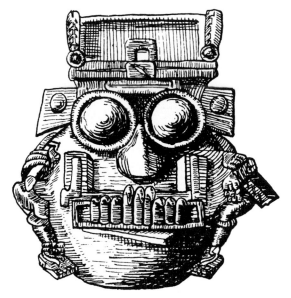

Figure of *Tlalok* from Tlaxcala. *Origins*

Mayan representations of rain. *Origins*

Decoration from an ancient Mayan vase. *Origins*

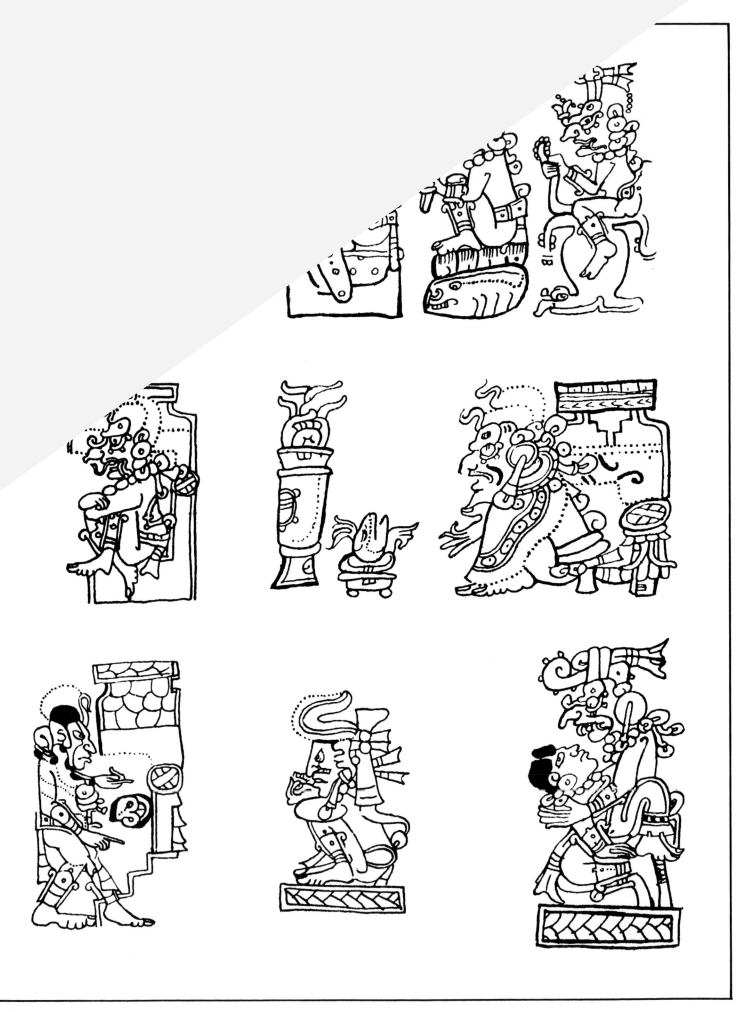

Mayan glyphs of *sipatli. Origins*

Mayan wall carving of the plumed
serpent *Kukulcan.* *Design and Decoration*

Mexican serpent design showing Mayan influence.
Source unknown

Mayan neck ornament carved on shell.
Source unknown

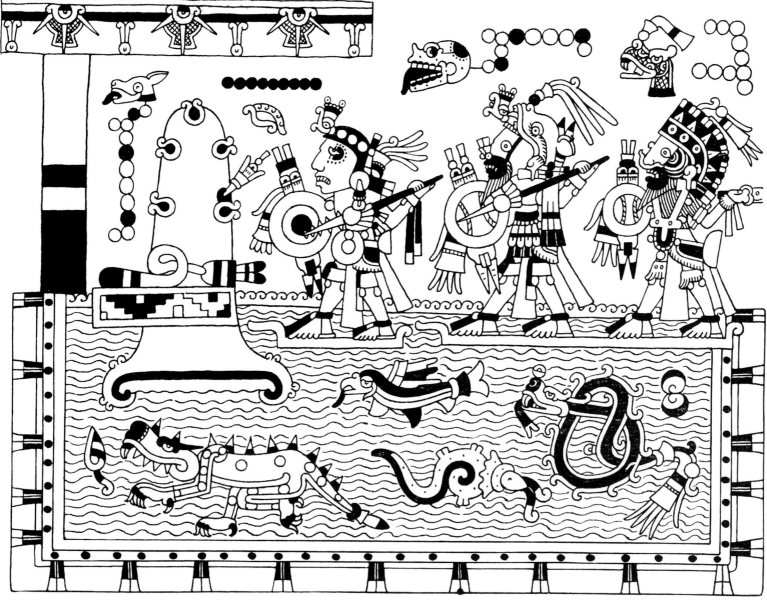

Painting from a Mixtec-Zapotec codex. *Design and Decoration*

Mexican Designs continued

Aztec calendar stone. *Design and Decoration*

 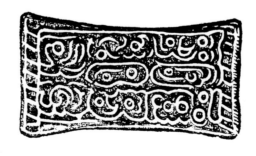 

Two earthen vessels and a decorative tablet, Mayan. *Source unknown*

Detail of a Mayan wall decoration. *Design and Decoration*

Mayan glyphs *tlalok* and *kiawitl. Origins*

Mexican Designs continued

Statue at Copan. *Century*

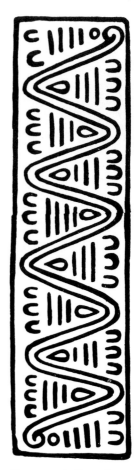

Representation of
the fire serpent.
Design Motifs

Stone slab of the
Totonac tribe.
Design and Decoration

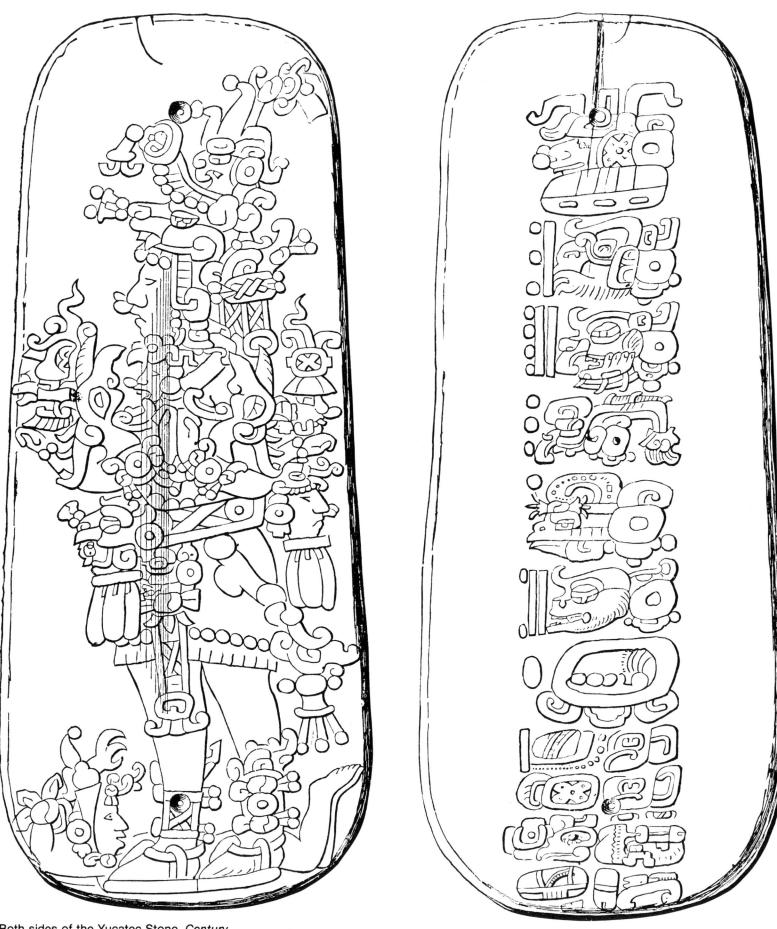

Both sides of the Yucatec Stone. *Century*

Modern Designs

Allover Patterns

Allover Patterns

Modern Designs continued

Patterns and Designs

Patterns and Designs

Modern Designs continued

Allover Patterns

Allover Patterns

Modern Designs continued

Patterns and Designs

Patterns and Designs

Modern Designs continued

Allover Patterns

Allover Patterns

Modern Designs continued

Patterns and Designs

Patterns and Designs

Modern Designs continued

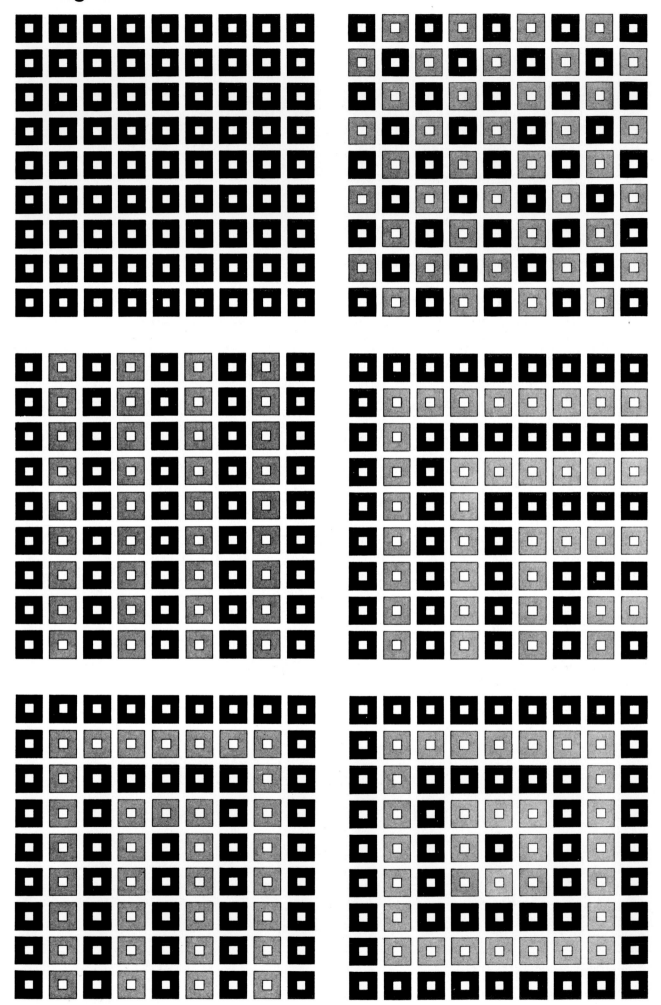

Patterns and Designs

Patterns and Designs

Modern Designs continued

Allover Patterns

Allover Patterns

Modern Designs continued

Patterns and Designs

Patterns and Designs

Modern Designs continued

Allover Patterns

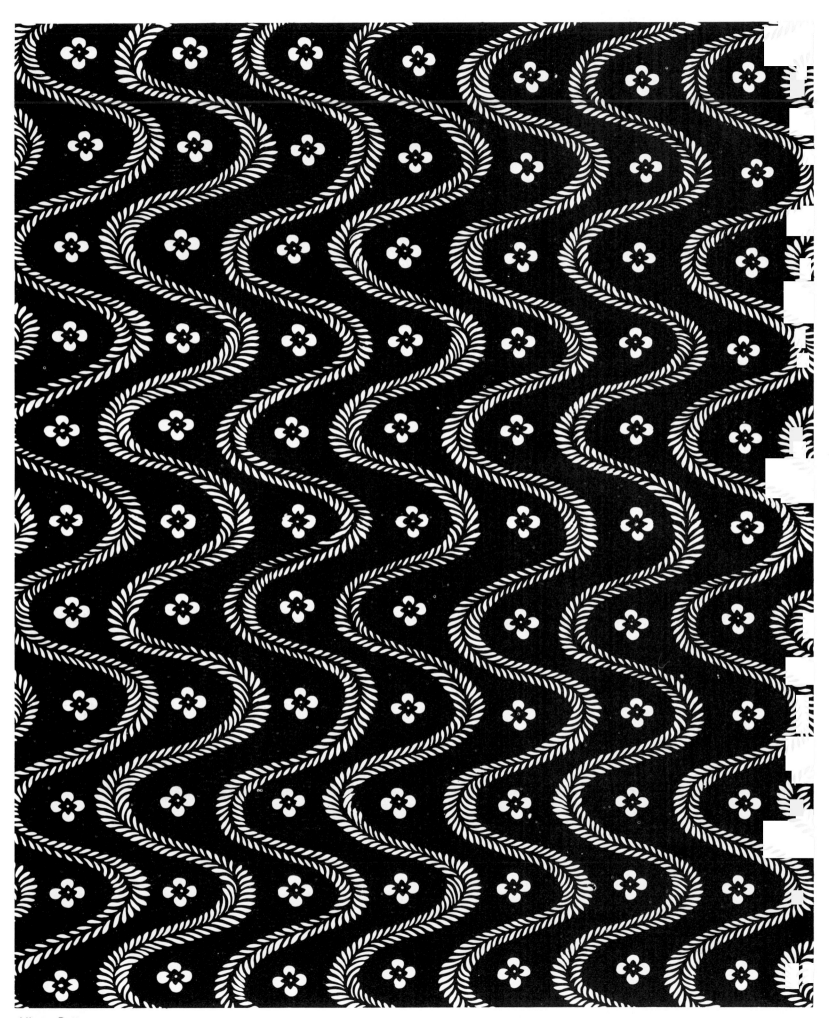

Allover Patterns

Nineteenth Century Glassware

Glass

Glass

Nineteenth Century Glassware continued

Glass

Nineteenth Century Glassware continued

Glass

Glass

Northwest Indian Designs

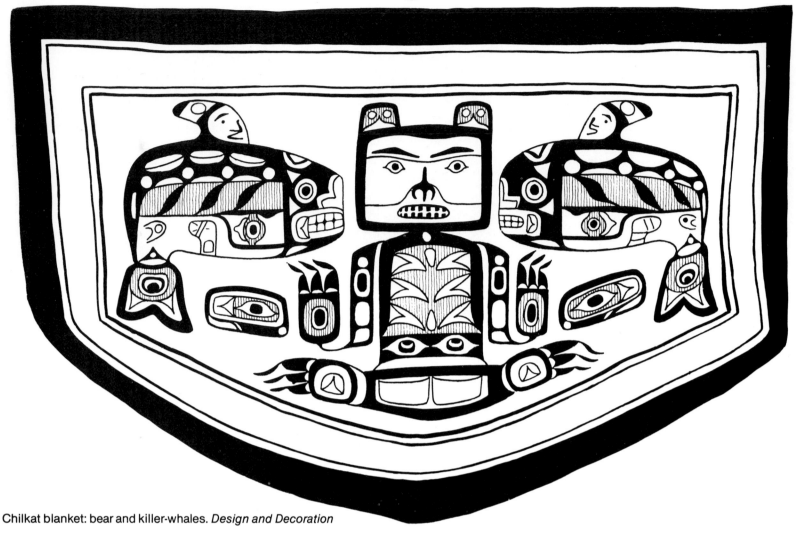

Chilkat blanket: bear and killer-whales. *Design and Decoration*

Haida designs. *Source unknown*

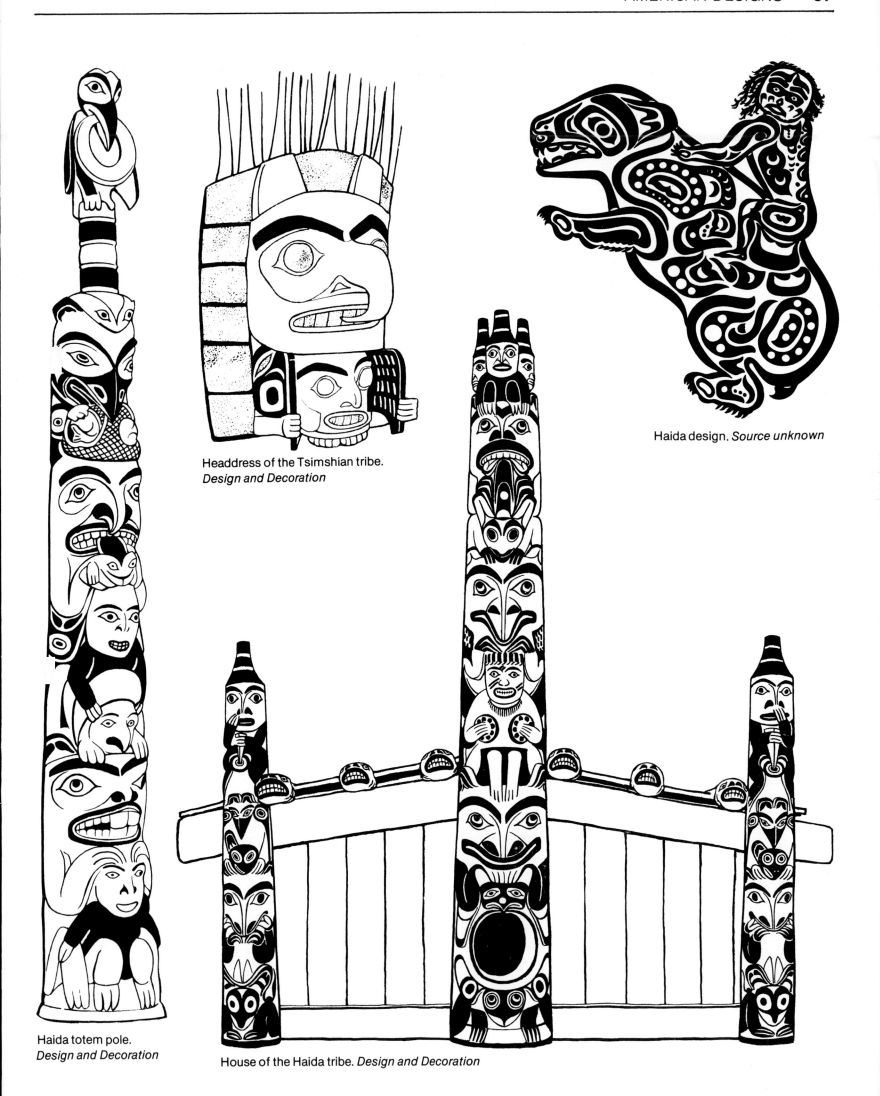

Headdress of the Tsimshian tribe.
Design and Decoration

Haida design. *Source unknown*

Haida totem pole.
Design and Decoration

House of the Haida tribe. *Design and Decoration*

Panamanian Designs

Vase with peccary form. *Ethnology*

Chiriquian statuette. *Ethnology*

Odd shaped vase. *Ethnology*

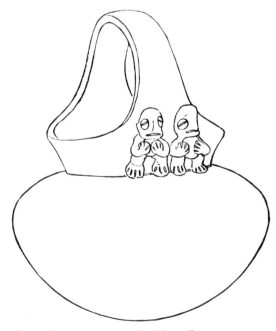

Chiriquian vase with arched handles. *Ethnology*

Chiriquian battle with arched panels. *Ethnology*

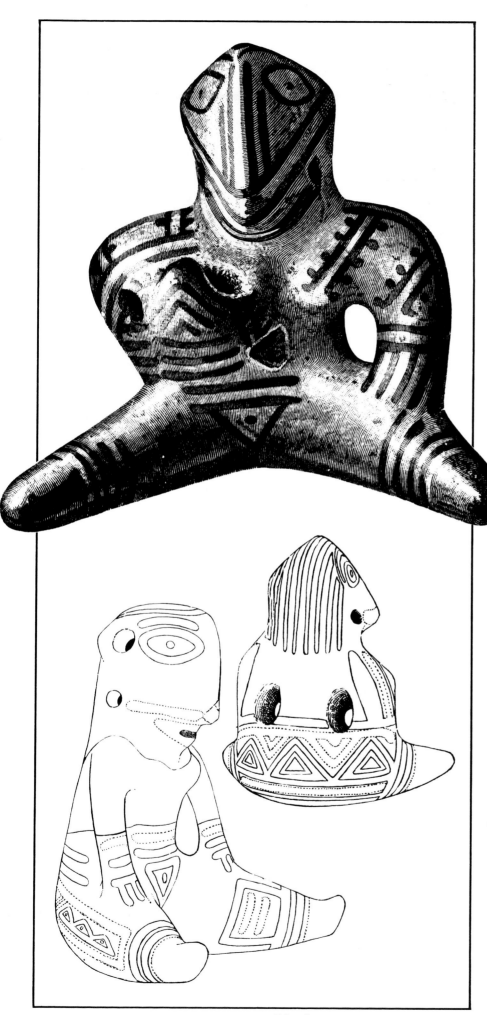

Underside of a vase. *Ethnology*

Chiriquian statuettes of the alligator group. *Ethnology*

Chiriquian vessel with relief of human figures. *Ethnology*

Panamanian Designs continued

Two Chiriquian double vessels. *Ethnology*

Chiriquian two-mouthed vase. *Ethnology*

Chiriquian vase and detail of its ornament. *Ethnology*

Large vase with high handles. *Ethnology*

Chiriquian vase. *Ethnology*

Chiriquian vase ornamented with grotesque heads. *Ethnology*

Chiriquian cup with animal-like legs. *Ethnology*

Chiriquian vase. *Ethnology*

Large vase with alligator designs.
Ethnology

Pennsylvania Dutch Designs

Sgraffito plate design. *Source unknown*

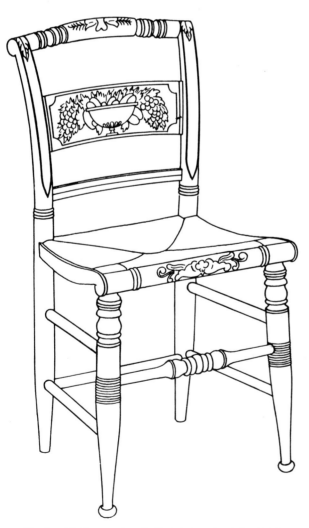

Chair with Pennsylvania Dutch inspired designs.
Source unknown

Various bird motifs. *Source unknown*

Decoration from a Pennsylvania Dutch chest. *Source unknown*

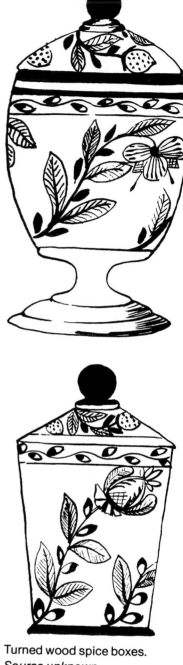

Turned wood spice boxes.
Source unknown

Marks of Pennsylvania Dutch craftsmen. *Source unknown*

Pennsylvania Designs continued

Pennsylvania Dutch hex signs and embroidery designs. *Symbols*

Design from a Pennsylvania Dutch plate. *Early American*

Pennsylvania Dutch design. *Early American*

Barn with hex signs, Lehigh County, Pennsylvania. *Source unknown*

Pennsylvania Dutch balloon-back chair. *Source unknown*

Pennsylvania Dutch spoon rack. *Source unknown*

Pennsylvania Designs continued

Design with birds and flowers. *Folk Art Motifs*

Various bird designs. *Folk Art Motifs*

Pennsylvania Designs continued

Pennsylvania Dutch flower decoration. *Folk Art Motifs*

Pennsylvania Dutch design with bird and flowers. *Folk Art Motifs*

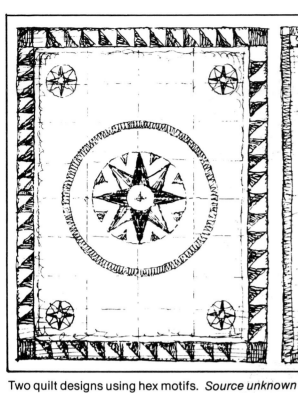
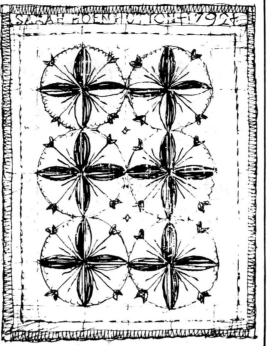

Two quilt designs using hex motifs. *Source unknown*

Flower ornament, Pennsylvania Dutch.
Early American

Conventional tulip design of the Pennsylvania Dutch. *Early American*

Pennsylvania Dutch sconce design, tulip. *Source unknown*

Pennsylvania Designs continued

Various human and floral designs. *Folk Art Motifs*

Pennsylvania Dutch flower design. *Early American*

Pennsylvania Dutch dower chest panel. *Source unknown*

Pennsylvania Dutch flower design. *Early American*

Hex sign. *Folk Art Motifs*

Pennsylvania Designs continued

Pennsylvania Dutch carvings, either butter or cookie molds. *Applied Arts*

Pennsylvania Dutch hex signs. *Folk Art Motifs*

Peruvian Designs

Pre-Columbian pottery piece from Nazca, Peru. *Das Ornament Werk* □

Peruvian costume
and makeup design.
Source unknown □

Costume design from the Peruvian Andes. *Source unknown* □

Pre-Columbian pottery piece from Nazca, Peru.
Das Ornament Werk □

Peruvian textile design. *Source unknown* □

Pre-Columbian textile design from Candevilla, Peru.
Das Ornament Werk □

Costume design from Lake Titicaca. *Source unknown* □

Costume design from Lake Titicaca.
Source unknown □

Pre-Columbian Peruvian pottery. *Das Ornament Werk* □

Peruvian Designs continued

Assorted Chimu vases. *I.L.E.*

Assorted Chimu vases. *I.L.E.*

Peruvian Designs continued

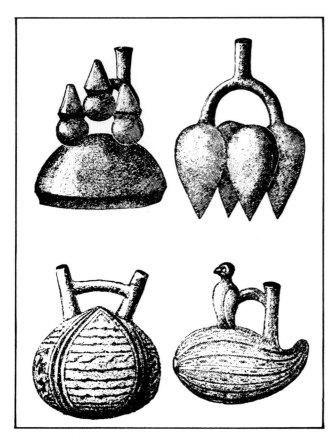

Peruvian ceramics. *American Continent*

Ornamental block of stone from a Peruvian temple. *Source unknown*

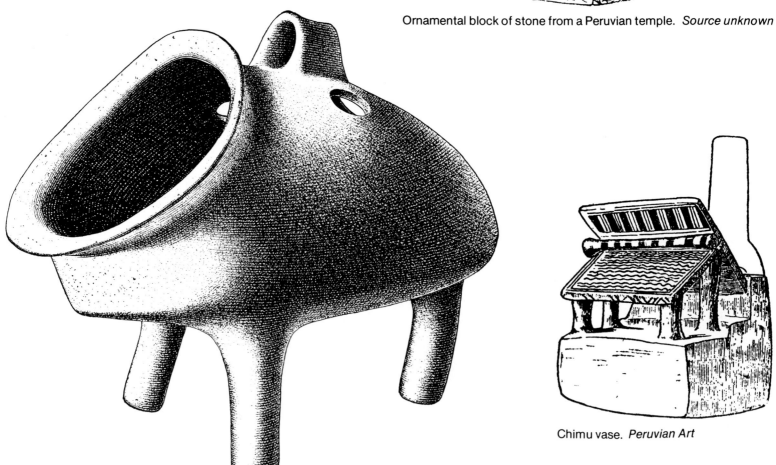

Chimu vase. *Peruvian Art*

Three-legged brazier from Machu Picchu. *Source unknown*

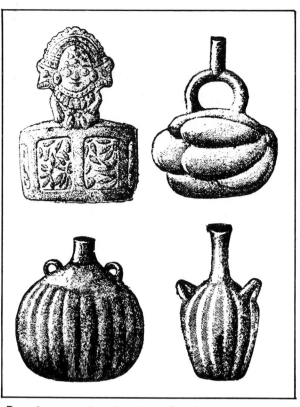

Peruvian ceramics. *American Continent*

Two-handled dish used by Incas to serve food. *Source unknown*

Chimu portrait vases. *Peruvian Art*

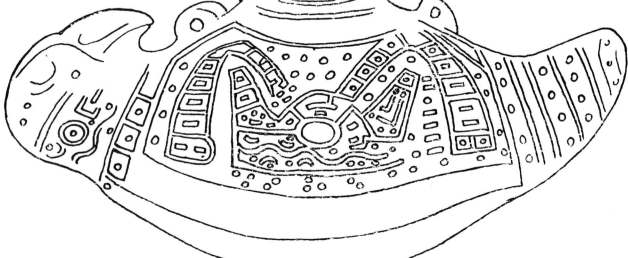

Typical vase from Recuay. *Source unknown*

Peruvian Designs continued

Dragon design from a painted pitcher, Truxillo. *Source unknown*

Peruvian design. *Source unknown*

Design from bowls of Nazca, Peru. *Source unknown*

Peruvian design. *Source unknown*

Peruvian design. *Source unknown*

Peruvian Designs continued

Peruvian designs based on the form of the puma. *Natural History*

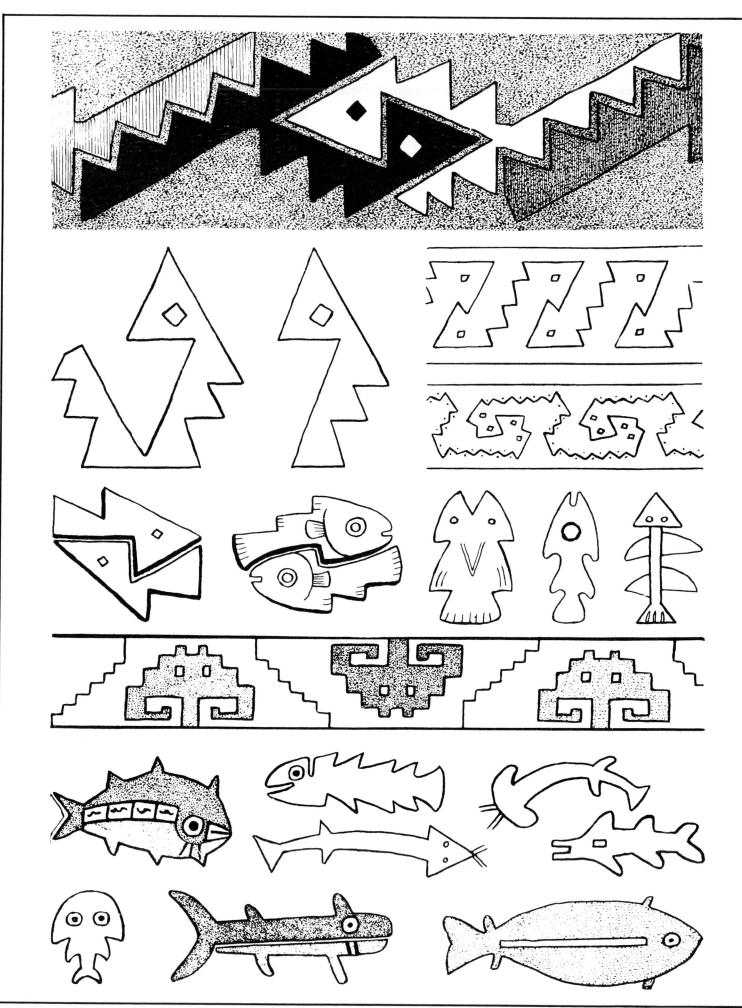

Peruvian designs based on the form of the fish. *Natural History*

Southwest Indian Designs

Modern Hopi potter design. *Decorative Art*

Pottery design from Sia, New Mexico. *Decorative Art*

Pueblo pottery design. *Decorative Art*

Painted vessel
of the Pueblos.
Source unknown

Painted vessel of the Pueblos.
Source unknown

Earthenware figure
of the Pueblos. *Source unknown*

Earthenware figure
of the Pueblos.
Source unknown

Pueblo pottery design, based on corn blades. *Decorative Art*

Pueblo pottery design. *Decorative Art*

Design from piece of pottery found in Utah. *Authentic Indian Designs*

Water vase of the Zuni tribe. *Authentic Indian Designs*

Pueblo pottery design. *Decorative Art*

Pueblo pottery design from Tusayan. *Authentic Indian Designs*

Weaving design of Maricopa tribe. *Decorative Art*

Modern Hopi pottery design. *Decorative Art*

Conventionalized border pattern for Pueblo pottery. *Decorative Art*

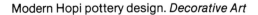

Southwest Indian Designs continued

Zuni pottery. *Ethnology*

Wolpi statuette and vase. *Ethnology*

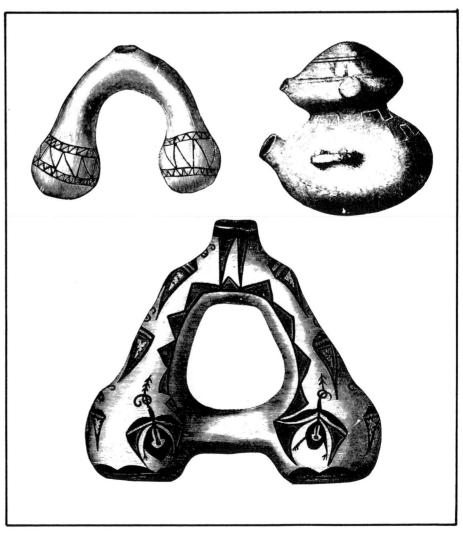

Wolpi water jars. *Ethnology*

Zuni canteens. *Ethnology*

Southwest Indian Designs continued

Zuni woman polishing pottery. *Ethnology*

Chiriquian alligator ware. *Ethnology*

Laguna water vessels. *Ethnology*

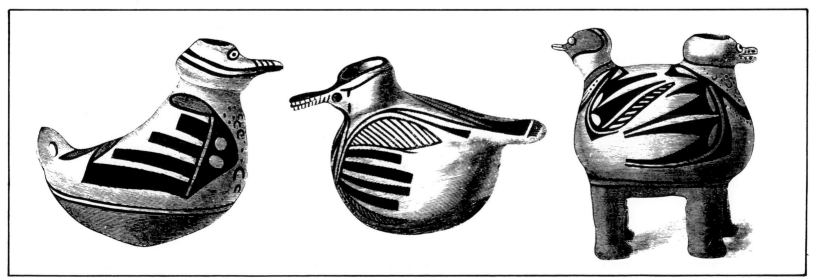

Laguna animal effigies. *Ethnology*

Wallpaper Designs

Wallpaper □

Wallpaper □

Wallpaper Designs continued

Wallpaper □

Wallpaper □

SOURCES

ALLOVER PATTERNS; full title, *Allover Patterns for Designers and Craftsmen.* New York: Dover Publications, Inc., 1975.

AMERICAN CONTINENT; full title, *The American Continent and Its Inhabitants Before Its Discovery by Columbus.* Cady, Annie Cole. Philadelphia: Gebbie, 1890.

APPLIED ARTS; from a portfolio of craft designs. No date.

AUTHENTIC INDIAN DESIGNS. Naylor, Maria, ed. New York: Dover Publications, Inc., 1975.

CENTURY; full title, *The Century Illustrated Monthly Magazine.* New York: The Century Company, 1889-1913.

DAS ORNAMENT WERK. Bossert, H. Th., ed. Berlin: Verlag Ernst Wasmuth GMBH, 1937.

DECORATIVE ART; full title, *Decorative Art of the Southwestern Indians.* Sides, Dorothy Smith. New York: Dover Publications, Inc., 1961.

DESIGN AND DECORATION; full title, *American Indian Design and Decoration.*

Appleton, Leroy H. New York: Dover Publications, Inc., 1971.

DESIGN MOTIFS; full title, *Design Motifs of Ancient Mexico.* Enciso, Jorge. New York: Dover Publications, Inc., 1953.

EARLY AMERICAN; full title, *Early American Design Motifs.* Chapman, Suzanne E. New York: Dover Publications, Inc., 1974.

ENCYCLOPÉDIE; full title, *Encyclopédie des Metiers d'Art.* Paris: Albert Morance, no date.

ETHNOLOGY; full title, *Bureau of Ethnology Annual Reports.* Washington, D.C.: Smithsonian Institution, c. 1895.

FOLK ART MOTIFS; full title, *Folk Art Motifs of Pennsylvania.* Lichten, Frances. New York: Dover Publications, Inc., 1954.

GLASS; full title, *Early American Pressed Glass Patterns.* Lee, Ruth Webb. Northboro, Mass.: Ruth Webb Lee, c. 1931.

I.L.E.; full title, *Illustracion Espanola y Americana.* Madrid, c. 1860.

INCIDENTS; full title, *Incidents of Travel in Central America, Chiapas, and Yucatan.* New York: Harpers, 1841.

LOTHROP; full title, *Pottery of Costa Rica and Nicaragua.* Lothrop, S.K. New York: Museum of the American Indian, 1926.

NATURAL HISTORY; full title, *American Museum Journal.* New York: The American Museum of Natural History, c. 1900.

ORIGINS; full title, *Mayan and Mexican Origins.* Cambridge, Mass.: privately printed, 1926.

PATTERNS AND DESIGNS; full title, *Optical and Geometrical Patterns and Designs.* New York: Dover Publications, Inc., 1970.

PERUVIAN ART; full title, *Peruvian Art in the School.* Izcue, Elena. Paris: Editorial Excelsior, 1926.

SYMBOLS; full title, *American Symbols.* Lehner, Ernst, compiler. New York, William Penn Publishing Corp., 1966.

WALLPAPER; full title, *Wards Wallpaper Catalog.* Baltimore, Md.: Montgomery Ward, c. 1950.